Jazz Play-Along

Book and CD for B♭, E♭, C and Bass Clef Instruments

Volume 168

Arranged and Produced by Mark Taylor

BOOK

CD

Cover photo © Herman Leonard Photography LLC

ISBN 978-1-4768-2125-2

7777 W. Bluemound Rd. P.O. Box 13819 Milwaukee, WI 53213

Visit Hal Leonard Online at
www.halleonard.com

TADD DAMERON

Volume 168

Arranged and Produced by
Mark Taylor

Featured Players:

Graham Breedlove–Trumpet
John Desalme–Tenor Sax
Tony Nalker–Piano
Jim Roberts–Guitar
Regan Brough–Bass
Todd Harrison–Drums

Recorded at Bias Studios, Springfield, Virginia
Bob Dawson, Engineer

HOW TO USE THE CD:
Each song has <u>two</u> tracks:

1) Split Track/Melody

Woodwind, Brass, Keyboard, and **Mallet Players** can use this track as a learning tool for melody style and inflection.

Bass Players can learn and perform with this track – remove the recorded bass track by turning down the volume on the LEFT channel.

Keyboard and **Guitar Players** can learn and perform with this track – remove the recorded piano part by turning down the volume on the RIGHT channel.

2) Full Stereo Track

Soloists or **Groups** can learn and perform with this accompaniment track with the RHYTHM SECTION only.

FOCUS

BY TADD DAMERON

CD
❶ : SPLIT TRACK/MELODY
❷ : FULL STEREO TRACK

C VERSION

GNID

CD

③ : SPLIT TRACK/MELODY
④ : FULL STEREO TRACK

BY TADD DAMERON

C VERSION

G7 Gb7 FMA7 N.C. BMI7(b5) Bb7
F6/A Ab7 TO CODA G7 C+7(#9) FMA7
DRUMS
SOLOS (2 CHORUSES)
F6 Eb7 F6 Eb7 FMA7 AMI7(b5) D+7(b9) GMI7 AMI7 D+7(b9)
G7 G+7 GMI7 C7(b9) F6 Eb7 F6 Eb7 FMA7
AMI7(b5) D+7(b9) GMI7 AMI7 D+7(b9) G7 C7 F6 CMI7 F+7(b9)
BbMI7 Eb7 AbMA7 F7 BbMI7 A7(b5) AbMA7 DMI7 G7 C6 A7
DMI7 G7 GMI7 C7(b9) F6 Eb7 F6 Eb7 FMA7
D.S. AL CODA
AMI7(b5) D+7(b9) GMI7 AMI7 D+7(b9) G7 C7 F6 CMI7 F+7(b9)
CODA
G7 C+7(#9) FMA7
DRUMS

GOOD BAIT

BY TADD DAMERON
AND COUNT BASIE

C VERSION

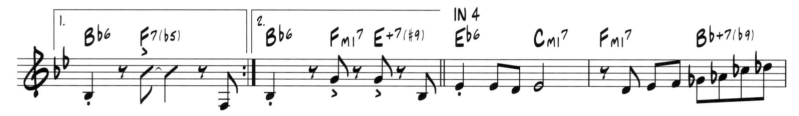

IN 4
SOLOS (2 CHORUSES)

| Bb6 | Gmi7 | Cmi7 | F+7(b9) | Dmi7 | G+7(b9) | Cmi7 | F+7(b9) |

| Bb7 | /D | EbMA7 | Ab7 | Dmi7 Dbmi7 Cmi7 Cb7 | Bb6 | F7(b5) |

| Bb6 | Gmi7 | Cmi7 | F+7(b9) | Dmi7 | G+7(b9) | Cmi7 | F+7(b9) |

| Bb7 | /D | EbMA7 | Ab7 | Dmi7 Dbmi7 Cmi7 Cb7 | Bb6 | Fmi7 Bb7(b9) |

| Eb6 | Cmi7 | Fmi7 | Bb+7(b9) | Gmi7 | C7(b9) | Fmi7 | Bb7(b9) |

| Eb7 | A7(b9) | AbMA7 | Db7 | Gmi7 Gbmi7 Fmi7 E7 | Eb6 | Gb7 F7 |

| Bb6 | Gmi7 | Cmi7 | F+7(b9) | Dmi7 | G+7(b9) | Cmi7 | F+7(b9) |

D.S. AL CODA
TAKE REPEAT

| Bb7 | /D | EbMA7 | Ab7 | Dmi7 Dbmi7 Cmi7 Cb7 | Bb6 | F7(b5) |

LAST X ONLY

⊕ CODA Bb6   F7(b5)

HOT HOUSE

BY TADD DAMERON

C VERSION

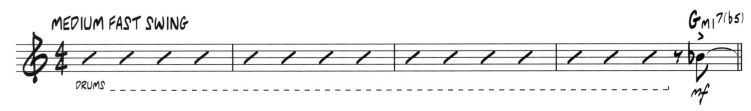

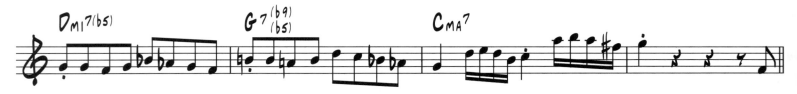

CD
9 : SPLIT TRACK/MELODY
10 : FULL STEREO TRACK

IF YOU COULD SEE ME NOW

LYRIC BY CARL SIGMAN
MUSIC BY TADD DAMERON

C VERSION

MEDIUM BALLAD

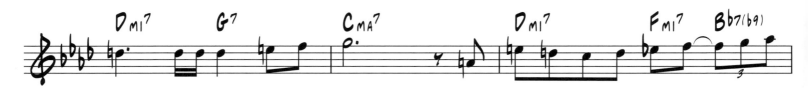

13

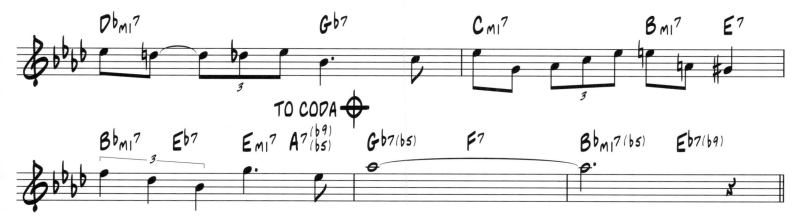

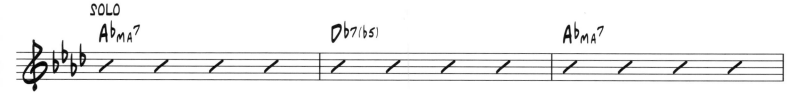

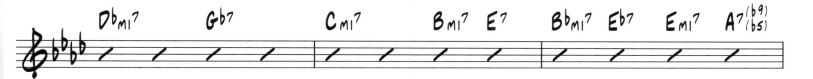

OUR DELIGHT

BY TADD DAMERON

C VERSION

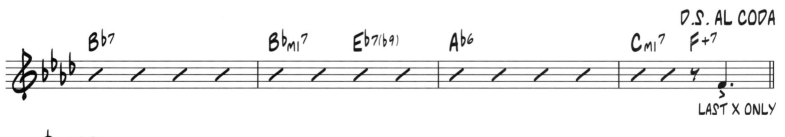

SID'S DELIGHT

BY TADD DAMERON

CD
15 : SPLIT TRACK/MELODY
16 : FULL STEREO TRACK

C VERSION

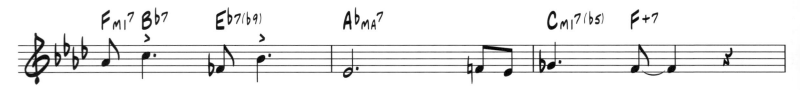

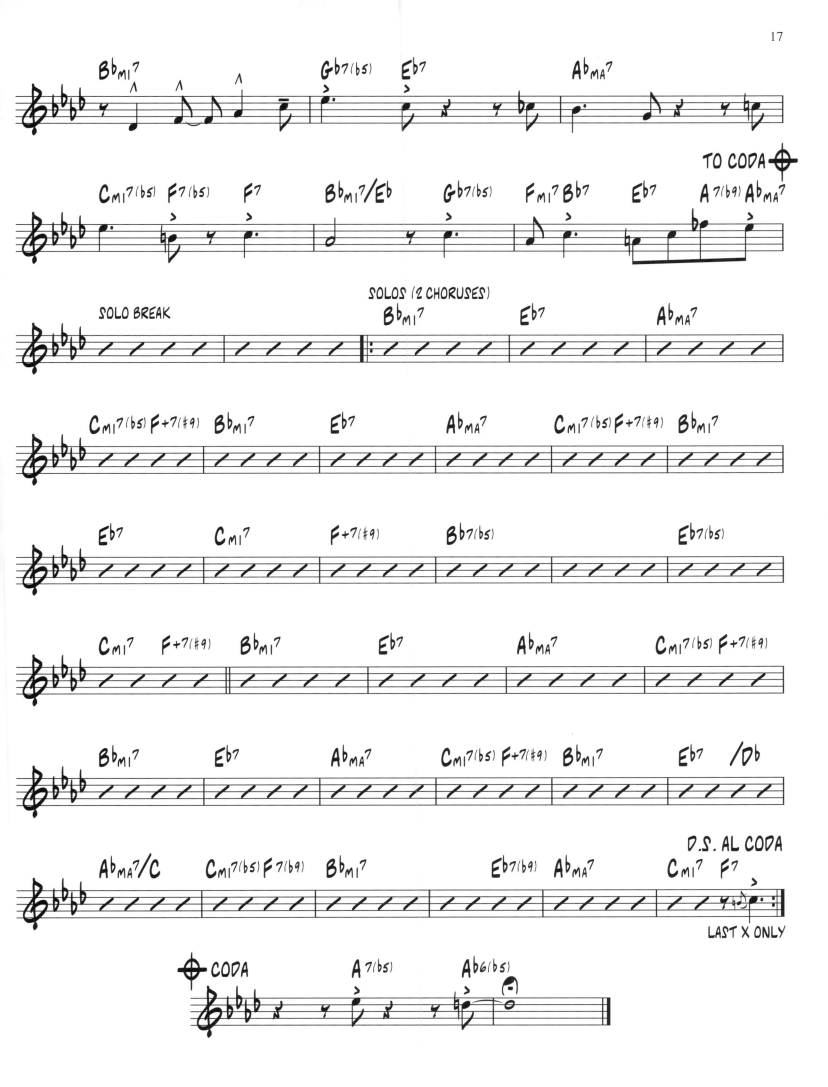

SOULTRANE

BY TADD DAMERON

C VERSION

MEDIUM BALLAD

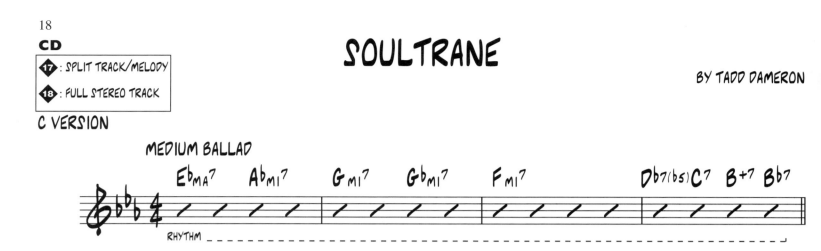

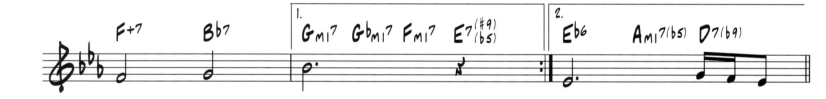

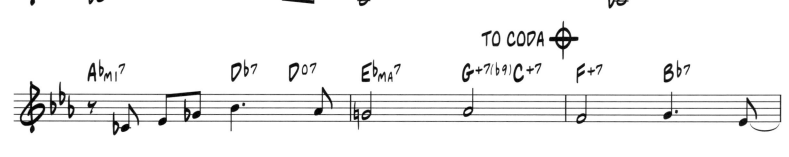

CD

◆19 : SPLIT TRACK/MELODY
◆20 : FULL STEREO TRACK

SUPER JET

BY TADD DAMERON

C VERSION

UPTEMPO SWING

DRUMS

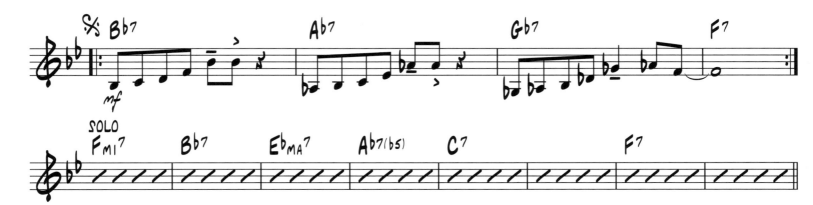

SOLO

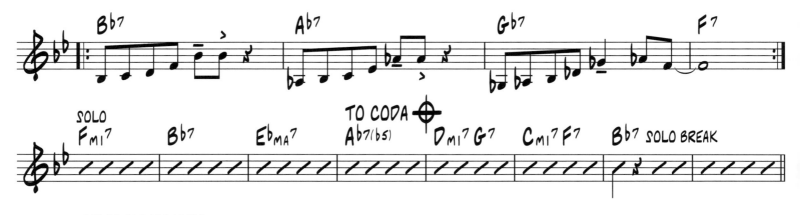

SOLO

TO CODA ⊕

SOLOS (3 CHORUSES)

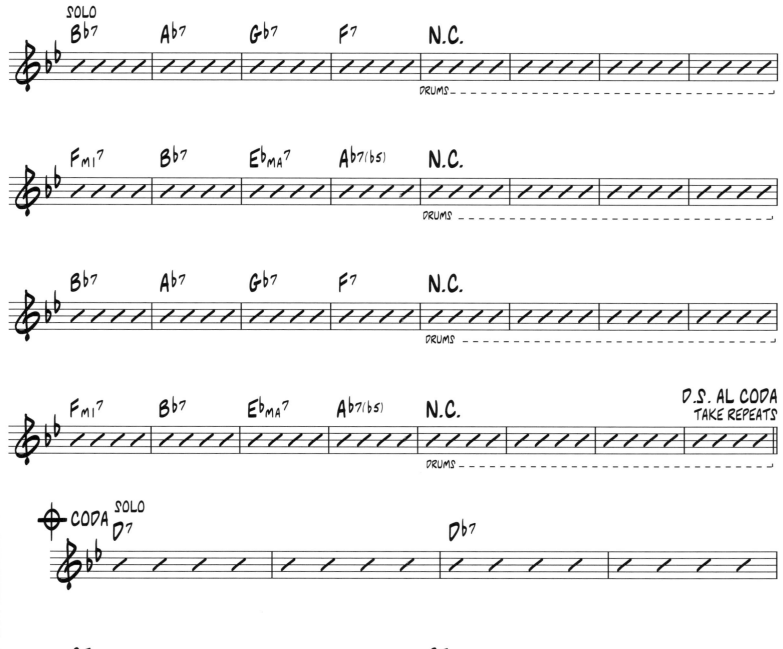

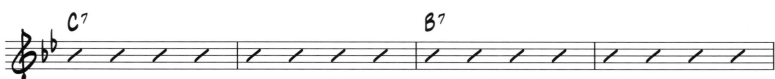

LADY BIRD

BY TADD DAMERON

C VERSION

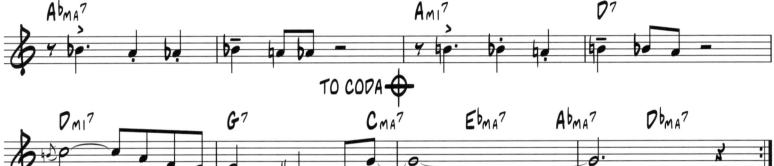

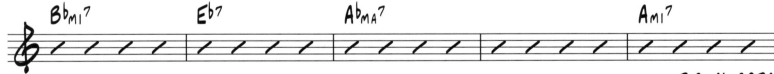

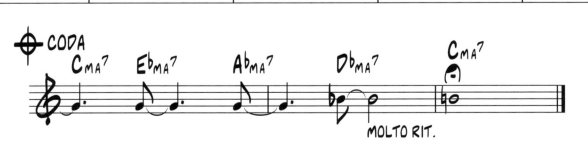

LADY BIRD

BY TADD DAMERON

CD
- 11 : SPLIT TRACK/MELODY
- 12 : FULL STEREO TRACK

Bb VERSION

BRIGHT SWING

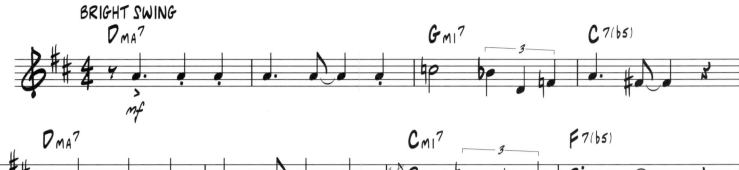

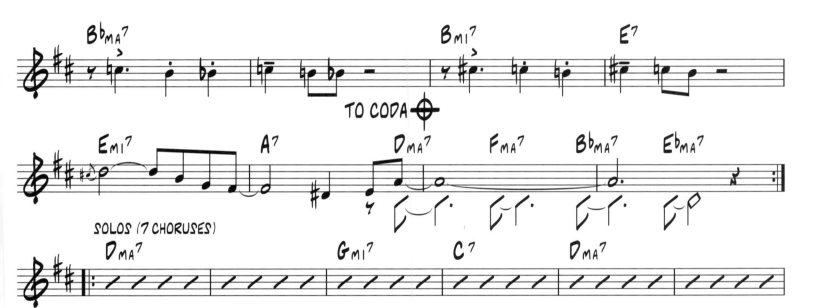

SOLOS (7 CHORUSES)

D.C. AL CODA
TAKE REPEAT

CODA

MOLTO RIT.

FOCUS

BY TADD DAMERON

Bb VERSION

GNID

BY TADD DAMERON

CD
- ❸ : SPLIT TRACK/MELODY
- ❹ : FULL STEREO TRACK

Bb VERSION — MEDIUM SWING

A7 Ab7 GMA7 N.C. C#MI7(b5) C7
G6/B Bb7 TO CODA A7 D+7(#9) GMA7
DRUMS
SOLOS (2 CHORUSES)
G6 F7 G6 F7 GMA7 BMI7(b5) E+7(b9) AMI7 BMI7 E+7(b9)
A7 A+7 AMI7 D7(b9) G6 F7 G6 F7 GMA7
BMI7(b5) E+7(b9) AMI7 BMI7 E+7(b9) A7 D7 G6 DMI7 G+7(b9)
CMI7 F7 BbMA7 G7 CMI7 B7(b5) BbMA7 EMI7 A7 D6 B7
EMI7 A7 AMI7 D7(b9) G6 F7 G6 F7 GMA7
D.S. AL CODA
BMI7(b5) E+7(b9) AMI7 BMI7 E+7(b9) A7 D7 G6 DMI7 G+7(b9)
CODA
A7 D+7(#9) GMA7
DRUMS

GOOD BAIT

BY TADD DAMERON
AND COUNT BASIE

CD

5 : SPLIT TRACK/MELODY
6 : FULL STEREO TRACK

Bb VERSION

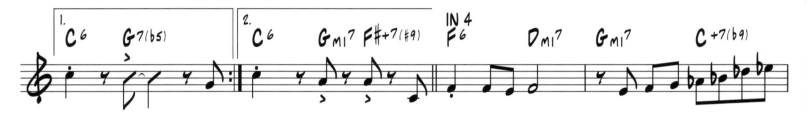

IN 4
SOLOS (2 CHORUSES)

| C⁶ | Aᴍɪ⁷ | Dᴍɪ⁷ | G⁺⁷⁽ᵇ⁹⁾ | Eᴍɪ⁷ | A⁺⁷⁽ᵇ⁹⁾ | Dᴍɪ⁷ | G⁺⁷⁽ᵇ⁹⁾ |

| C⁷ | /E | Fᴍᴀ⁷ | B♭⁷ | Eᴍɪ⁷ E♭ᴍɪ⁷ Dᴍɪ⁷ D♭⁷ | C⁶ | G⁷⁽ᵇ⁵⁾ |

| C⁶ | Aᴍɪ⁷ | Dᴍɪ⁷ | G⁺⁷⁽ᵇ⁹⁾ | Eᴍɪ⁷ | A⁺⁷⁽ᵇ⁹⁾ | Dᴍɪ⁷ | G⁺⁷⁽ᵇ⁹⁾ |

| C⁷ | /E | Fᴍᴀ⁷ | B♭⁷ | Eᴍɪ⁷ E♭ᴍɪ⁷ Dᴍɪ⁷ D♭⁷ | C⁶ | Gᴍɪ⁷ C⁷⁽ᵇ⁹⁾ |

| F⁶ | Dᴍɪ⁷ | Gᴍɪ⁷ | C⁺⁷⁽ᵇ⁹⁾ | Aᴍɪ⁷ | D⁷⁽ᵇ⁹⁾ | Gᴍɪ⁷ | C⁷⁽ᵇ⁹⁾ |

| F⁷ | B⁷⁽ᵇ⁹⁾ | B♭ᴍᴀ⁷ | E♭⁷ | Aᴍɪ⁷ A♭ᴍɪ⁷ Gᴍɪ⁷ F♯⁷ | F⁶ | A♭⁷ G⁷ |

| C⁶ | Aᴍɪ⁷ | Dᴍɪ⁷ | G⁺⁷⁽ᵇ⁹⁾ | Eᴍɪ⁷ | A⁺⁷⁽ᵇ⁹⁾ | Dᴍɪ⁷ | G⁺⁷⁽ᵇ⁹⁾ |

D.S. AL CODA
TAKE REPEAT

| C⁷ | /E | Fᴍᴀ⁷ | B♭⁷ | Eᴍɪ⁷ E♭ᴍɪ⁷ Dᴍɪ⁷ D♭⁷ | C⁶ | G⁷⁽ᵇ⁵⁾ |

LAST X ONLY

⊕ CODA
C⁶   G⁷⁽ᵇ⁵⁾

HOT HOUSE

BY TADD DAMERON

Bb VERSION

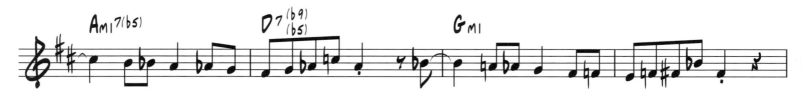

FINE

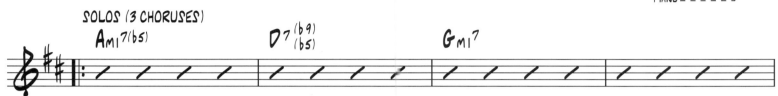

SOLOS (3 CHORUSES)

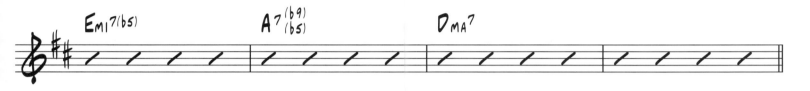

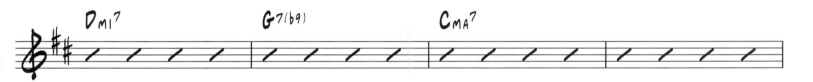

D.S. AL FINE

LAST X ONLY

IF YOU COULD SEE ME NOW

CD
- 9 : SPLIT TRACK/MELODY
- 10 : FULL STEREO TRACK

LYRIC BY CARL SIGMAN
MUSIC BY TADD DAMERON

Bb VERSION

MEDIUM BALLAD

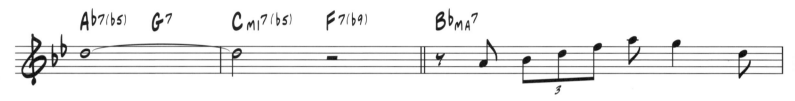

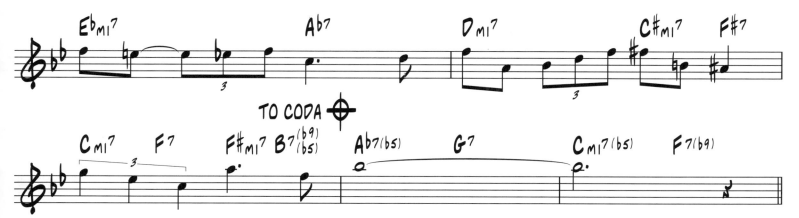

OUR DELIGHT

BY TADD DAMERON

CD
13 : SPLIT TRACK/MELODY
14 : FULL STEREO TRACK

Bb VERSION

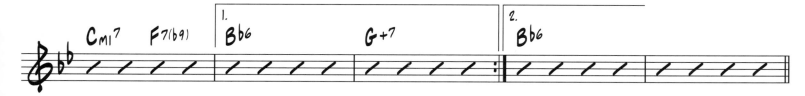

SID'S DELIGHT

BY TADD DAMERON

CD
- **15** : SPLIT TRACK/MELODY
- **16** : FULL STEREO TRACK

Bb VERSION

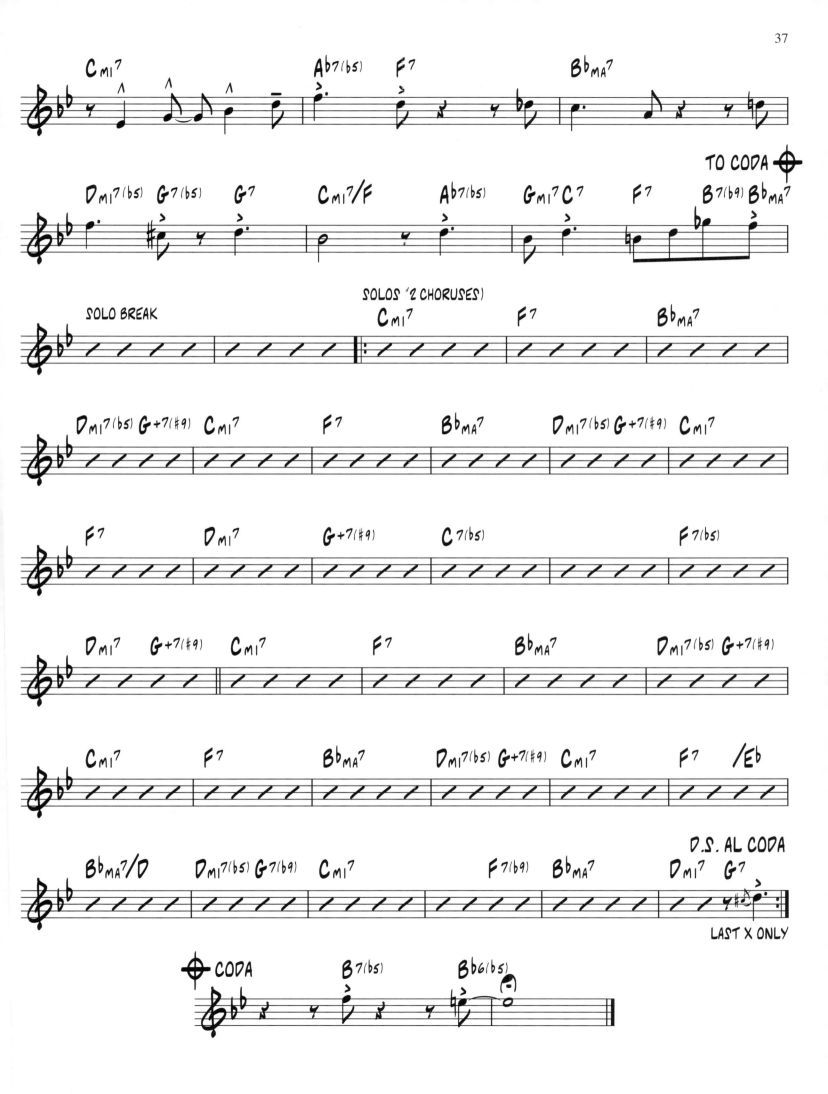

SOULTRANE

BY TADD DAMERON

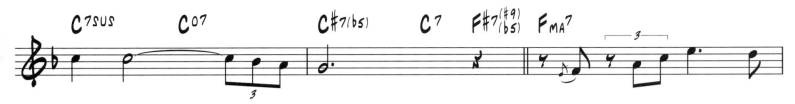

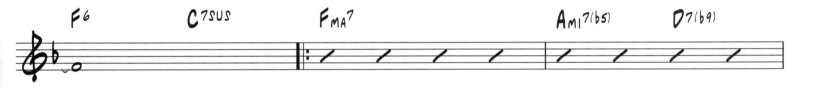

SUPER JET

BY TADD DAMERON

Bb VERSION

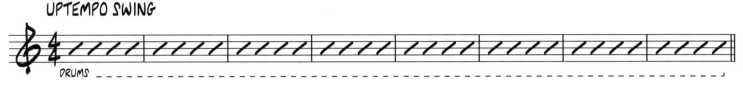

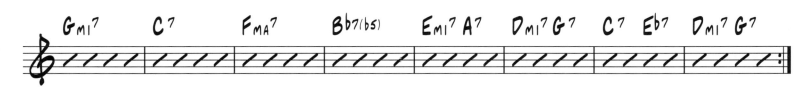

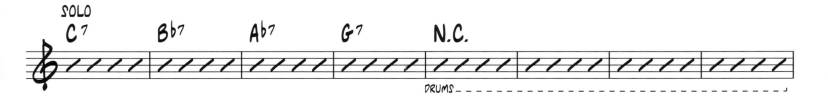

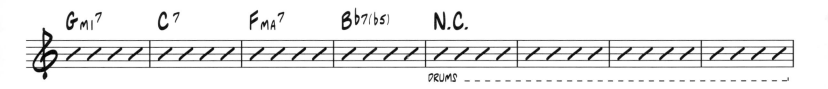

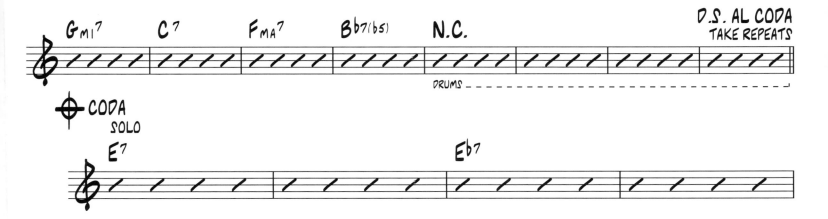

FOCUS

BY TADD DAMERON

CD

1 : SPLIT TRACK/MELODY
2 : FULL STEREO TRACK

Eb VERSION

CD

3 : SPLIT TRACK/MELODY
4 : FULL STEREO TRACK

GNID

BY TADD DAMERON

Eb VERSION

E7 Eb7 DMA7 N.C. G#MI7(b5) G7
D6/F# F7 TO CODA E7 A+7(#9) DMA7
DRUMS
SOLOS (2 CHORUSES)
D6 C7 D6 C7 DMA7 F#MI7(b5) B+7(b9) EMI7 F#MI7 B+7(b9)
E7 E+7 EMI7 A7(b9) D6 C7 D6 C7 DMA7
F#MI7(b5) B+7(b9) EMI7 F#MI7 B+7(b9) E7 A7 D6 AMI7 D+7(b9)
GMI7 C7 FMA7 D7 GMI7 F#7(b5) FMA7 BMI7 E7 A6 F#7
BMI7 E7 EMI7 A7(b9) D6 C7 D6 C7 DMA7
D.S. AL CODA
F#MI7(b5) B+7(b9) EMI7 F#MI7 B+7(b9) E7 A7 D6 AMI7 D+7(b9)
CODA E7 A+7(#9) DMA7
DRUMS

CD

5 : SPLIT TRACK/MELODY
6 : FULL STEREO TRACK

GOOD BAIT

BY TADD DAMERON
AND COUNT BASIE

Eb VERSION

MEDIUM SWING, IN 2

IN 2

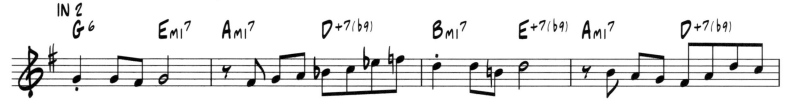

TO CODA ⊕

IN 4
SOLOS (2 CHORUSES)
G6 Emi7 Ami7 D+7(b9) Bmi7 E+7(b9) Ami7 D+7(b9)
G7 /B Cma7 F7 Bmi7 Bbmi7 Ami7 Ab7 G6 D7(b5)
G6 Emi7 Ami7 D+7(b9) Bmi7 E+7(b9) Ami7 D+7(b9)
G7 /B Cma7 F7 Bmi7 Bbmi7 Ami7 Ab7 G6 Dmi7 G7(b9)
C6 Ami7 Dmi7 G+7(b9) Emi7 A7(b9) Dmi7 G7(b9)
C7 F#7(b9) Fma7 Bb7 Emi7 Ebmi7 Dmi7 C#7 C6 Eb7 D7
G6 Emi7 Ami7 D+7(b9) Bmi7 E+7(b9) Ami7 D+7(b9)
D.S. AL CODA
TAKE REPEAT
G7 /B Cma7 F7 Bmi7 Bbmi7 Ami7 Ab7 G6 D7(b5)
LAST X ONLY
CODA G6 D7(b5)

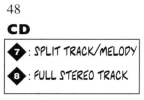

HOT HOUSE

BY TADD DAMERON

Eb VERSION

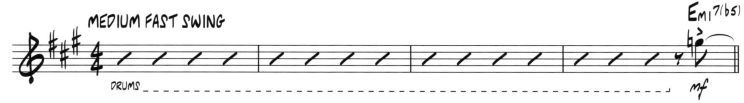

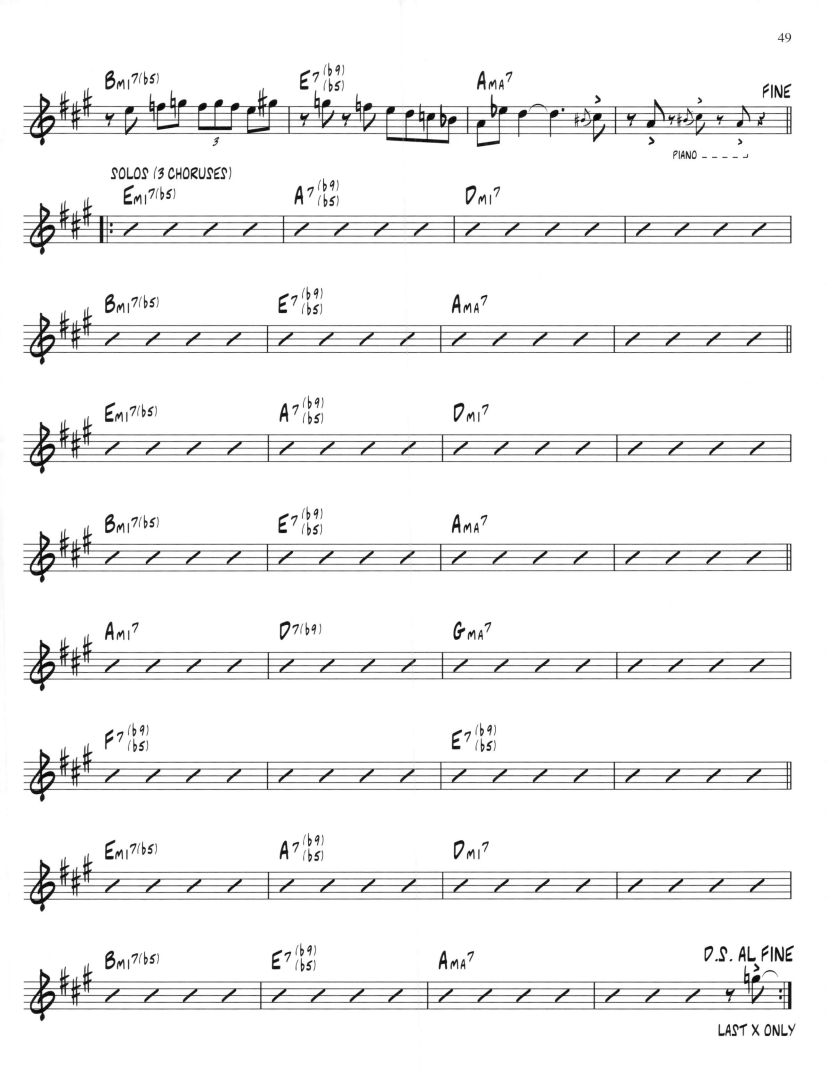

IF YOU COULD SEE ME NOW

LYRIC BY CARL SIGMAN
MUSIC BY TADD DAMERON

Eb VERSION

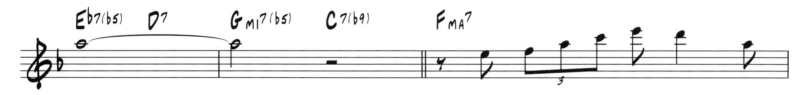

OUR DELIGHT

CD
◆13 : SPLIT TRACK/MELODY
◆14 : FULL STEREO TRACK

BY TADD DAMERON

Eb VERSION

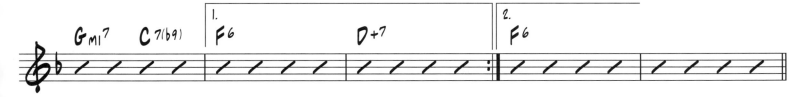

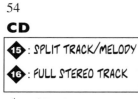

SID'S DELIGHT

BY TADD DAMERON

Eb VERSION

SOULTRANE

BY TADD DAMERON

CD

17 : SPLIT TRACK/MELODY
18 : FULL STEREO TRACK

Eb VERSION

MEDIUM BALLAD

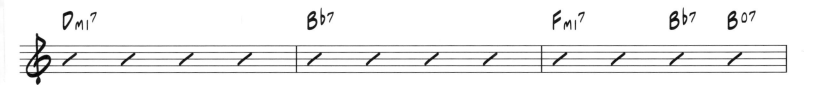

CD

19 : SPLIT TRACK/MELODY
20 : FULL STEREO TRACK

SUPER JET

BY TADD DAMERON

Eb VERSION

UPTEMPO SWING

DRUMS

SOLO

SOLO   TO CODA ⊕

SOLOS (3 CHORUSES)

Dmi7　G7　Cma7　F7(b5)　Bmi7 E7　Ami7 D7　G7 Bb7　Ami7 D7

SOLO

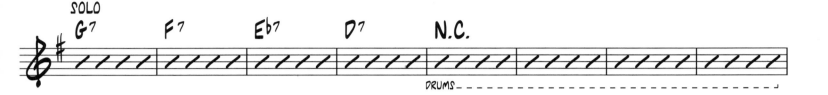

G7　F7　Eb7　D7　N.C.

DRUMS - - - - - - - - - - - -

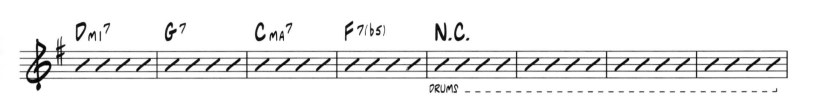

Dmi7　G7　Cma7　F7(b5)　N.C.

DRUMS - - - - - - - - - - - -

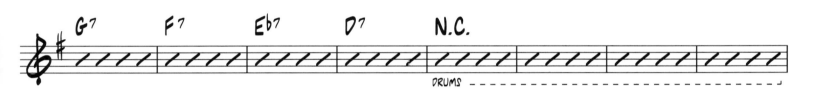

G7　F7　Eb7　D7　N.C.

DRUMS - - - - - - - - - - - -

D.S. AL CODA
TAKE REPEATS

Dmi7　G7　Cma7　F7(b5)　N.C.

DRUMS - - - - - - - - - - - -

CODA SOLO

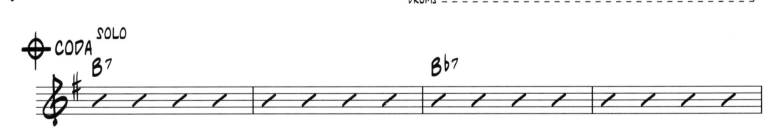

B7　　　　Bb7

A7　　　　G#7

G7　　　　　　　　　　　　G7(b5)

BREAK - - - - - - - - - - - -

Lady Bird

BY TADD DAMERON

Eb VERSION

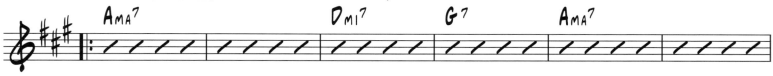

LADY BIRD

BY TADD DAMERON

FOCUS

BY TADD DAMERON

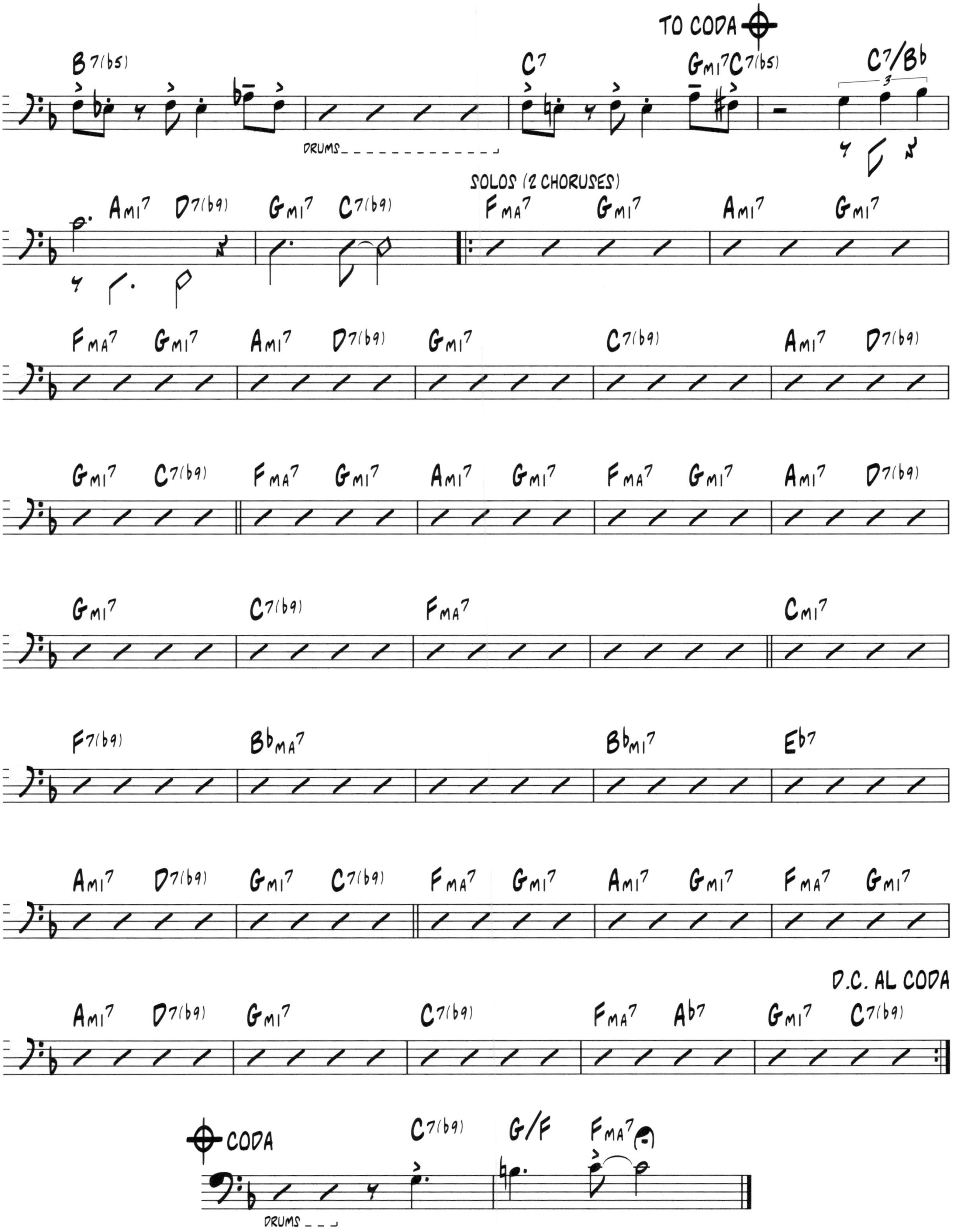
TO CODA
B7(b5)
C7
Gmi7 C7(b5)
C7/Bb
3
DRUMS
SOLOS (2 CHORUSES)
Ami7 D7(b9) Gmi7 C7(b9) Fma7 Gmi7 Ami7 Gmi7
Fma7 Gmi7 Ami7 D7(b9) Gmi7 C7(b9) Ami7 D7(b9)
Gmi7 C7(b9) Fma7 Gmi7 Ami7 Gmi7 Fma7 Gmi7 Ami7 D7(b9)
Gmi7 C7(b9) Fma7 Cmi7
F7(b9) Bbma7 Bbmi7 Eb7
Ami7 D7(b9) Gmi7 C7(b9) Fma7 Gmi7 Ami7 Gmi7 Fma7 Gmi7
D.C. AL CODA
Ami7 D7(b9) Gmi7 C7(b9) Fma7 Ab7 Gmi7 C7(b9)
CODA
C7(b9) G/F Fma7
DRUMS

GNID

CD
3 : SPLIT TRACK/MELODY
4 : FULL STEREO TRACK

BY TADD DAMERON

𝄢: C VERSION

GOOD BAIT

BY TADD DAMERON
AND COUNT BASIE

CD
5 : SPLIT TRACK/MELODY
6 : FULL STEREO TRACK

𝄢: C VERSION

MEDIUM SWING, IN 2

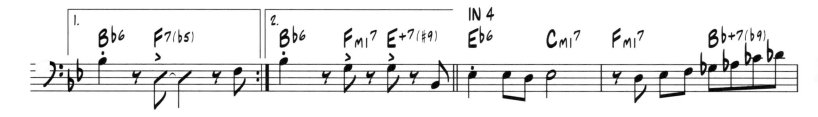

IN 2

TO CODA ⊕

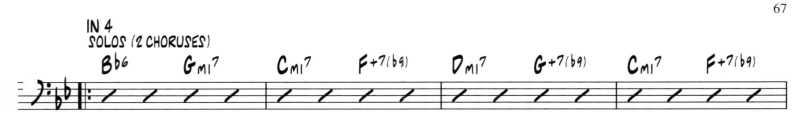

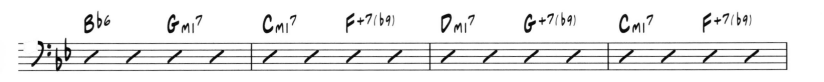

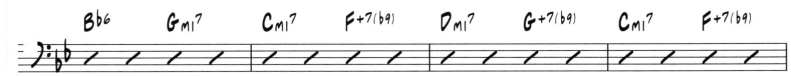

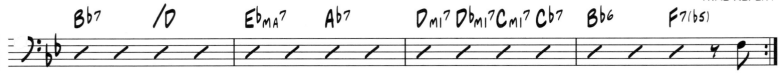

CD
◀ : SPLIT TRACK/MELODY
🔊 : FULL STEREO TRACK

HOT HOUSE

BY TADD DAMERON

𝄢: C VERSION

MEDIUM FAST SWING

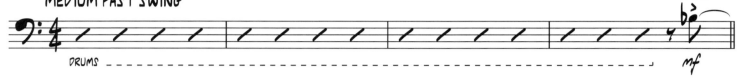

DRUMS

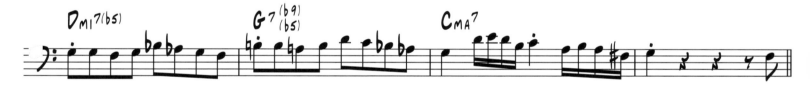

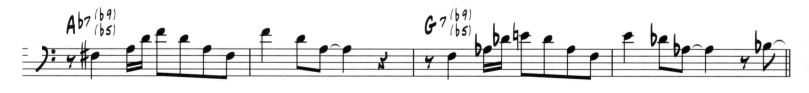

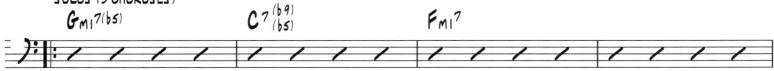

SOLOS (3 CHORUSES)

CD

⑨ : SPLIT TRACK/MELODY
⑩ : FULL STEREO TRACK

IF YOU COULD SEE ME NOW

LYRIC BY CARL SIGMAN
MUSIC BY TADD DAMERON

𝄢: C VERSION

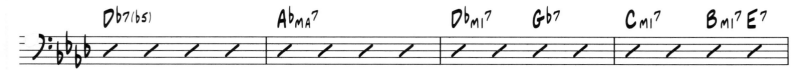

OUR DELIGHT

CD
13 : SPLIT TRACK/MELODY
14 : FULL STEREO TRACK

BY TADD DAMERON

🎼: C VERSION

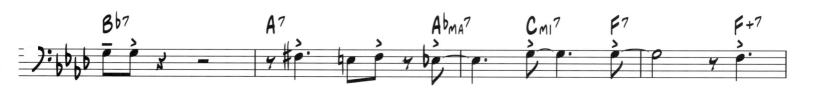

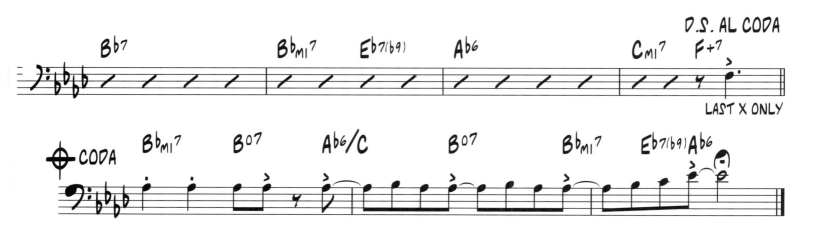

SID'S DELIGHT

BY TADD DAMERON

𝄢: C VERSION

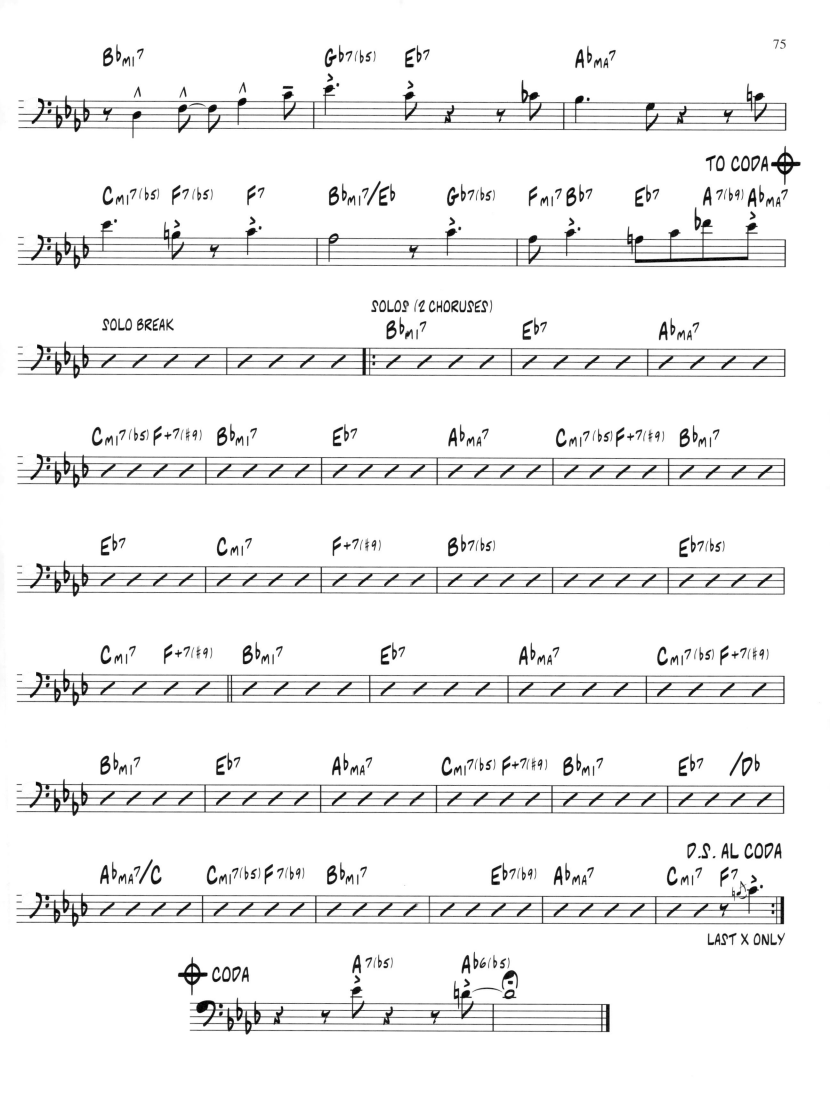

CD
17 : SPLIT TRACK/MELODY
18 : FULL STEREO TRACK

SOULTRANE

BY TADD DAMERON

𝄢: C VERSION

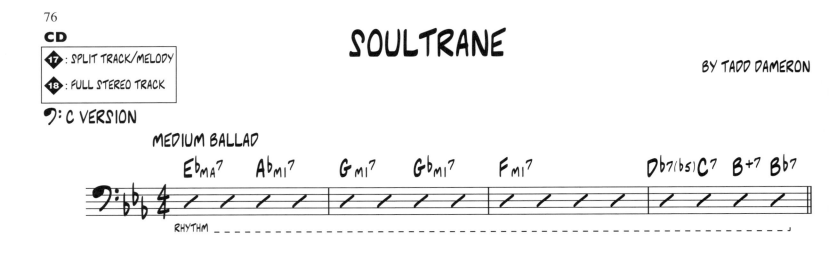

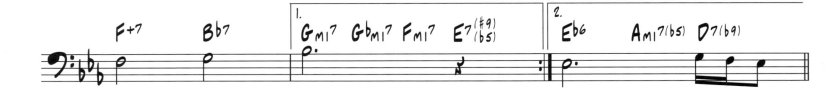

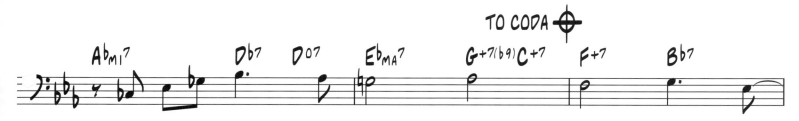

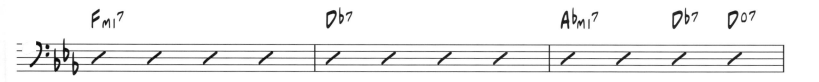

SUPER JET

BY TADD DAMERON

CD
◆19: SPLIT TRACK/MELODY
◆20: FULL STEREO TRACK

𝄢 C VERSION

UPTEMPO SWING

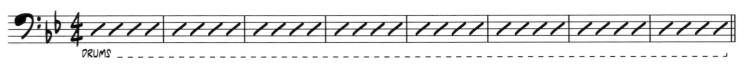

DRUMS —

𝄋 Bb7 · Ab7 · Gb7 · F7

mf

SOLO
Fmi7 · Bb7 · EbMA7 · Ab7(b5) · C7 · F7

Bb7 · Ab7 · Gb7 · F7

SOLO
Fmi7 · Bb7 · EbMA7 · Ab7(b5) · TO CODA ⊕ · Dmi7 G7 · Cmi7 F7 · Bb7 SOLO BREAK

SOLOS (3 CHORUSES)
Bb7 · Ab7 · Gb7 · F7 · Bb7 · Ab7 · Gb7 · F7

Fmi7 · Bb7 · EbMA7 · Ab7(b5) · C7 · F7

Bb7 · Ab7 · Gb7 · F7 · Bb7 · Ab7 · Gb7 · F7

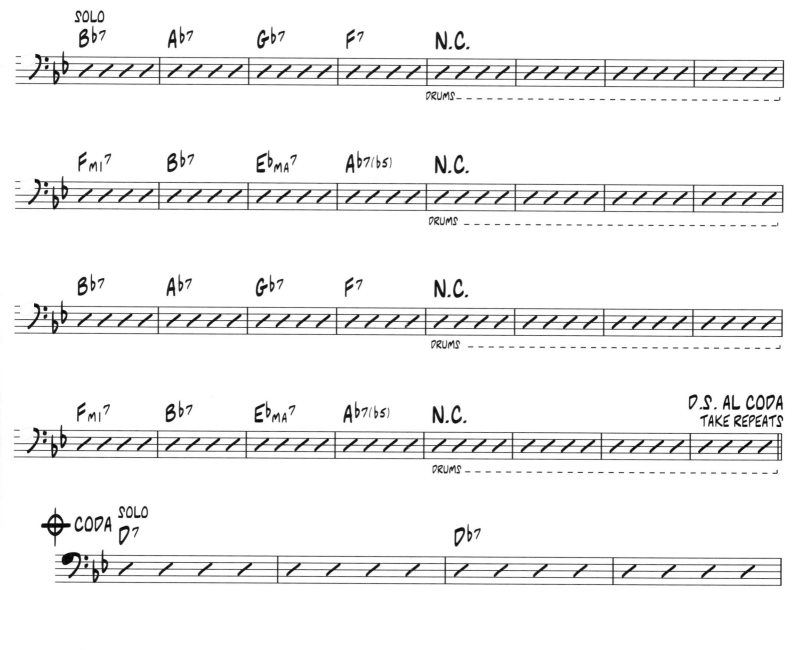
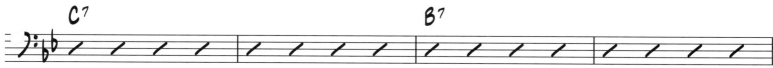

For use with all B-flat, E-flat, Bass Clef and C instruments, the Jazz Play-Along® Series is the ultimate learning tool for all jazz musicians. With musician-friendly lead sheets, melody cues, and other split-track choices on the included CD, these first-of-a-kind packages help you master improvisation while playing some of the greatest tunes of all time. FOR STUDY, each tune includes a split track with: melody cue with proper style and inflection • professional rhythm tracks • choruses for soloing • removable bass part • removable piano part. FOR PERFORMANCE, each tune also has: an additional full stereo accompaniment track (no melody) • additional choruses for soloing.

1A. MAIDEN VOYAGE/ALL BLUES
00843158 ....$15.99

1. DUKE ELLINGTON
00841644..............$16.95

2. MILES DAVIS
00841645..............$16.95

3. THE BLUES
00841646..............$16.99

4. JAZZ BALLADS
00841691..............$16.99

5. BEST OF BEBOP
00841689..............$16.95

6. JAZZ CLASSICS WITH EASY CHANGES
00841690..............$16.99

7. ESSENTIAL JAZZ STANDARDS
00843000..............$16.99

8. ANTONIO CARLOS JOBIM AND THE ART OF THE BOSSA NOVA
00843001..............$16.95

9. DIZZY GILLESPIE
00843002..............$16.99

10. DISNEY CLASSICS
00843003..............$16.99

11. RODGERS AND HART FAVORITES
00843004..............$16.99

12. ESSENTIAL JAZZ CLASSICS
00843005..............$16.99

13. JOHN COLTRANE
00843006..............$16.95

14. IRVING BERLIN
00843007..............$15.99

15. RODGERS & HAMMERSTEIN
00843008..............$15.99

16. COLE PORTER
00843009..............$15.95

17. COUNT BASIE
00843010..............$16.95

18. HAROLD ARLEN
00843011..............$15.95

19. COOL JAZZ
00843012..............$15.95

20. CHRISTMAS CAROLS
00843080..............$14.95

21. RODGERS AND HART CLASSICS
00843014..............$14.95

22. WAYNE SHORTER
00843015..............$16.95

23. LATIN JAZZ
00843016..............$16.95

24. EARLY JAZZ STANDARDS
00843017..............$14.95

25. CHRISTMAS JAZZ
00843018..............$16.95

26. CHARLIE PARKER
00843019..............$16.95

27. GREAT JAZZ STANDARDS
00843020..............$16.99

28. BIG BAND ERA
00843021..............$15.99

29. LENNON AND MCCARTNEY
00843022..............$16.95

30. BLUES' BEST
00843023..............$15.99

31. JAZZ IN THREE
00843024..............$15.99

32. BEST OF SWING
00843025..............$15.99

33. SONNY ROLLINS
00843029..............$15.95

34. ALL TIME STANDARDS
00843030..............$15.99

35. BLUESY JAZZ
00843031..............$16.99

36. HORACE SILVER
00843032..............$16.99

37. BILL EVANS
00843033..............$16.95

38. YULETIDE JAZZ
00843034..............$16.95

39. "ALL THE THINGS YOU ARE" & MORE JEROME KERN SONGS
00843035..............$15.99

40. BOSSA NOVA
00843036..............$16.99

41. CLASSIC DUKE ELLINGTON
00843037..............$16.99

42. GERRY MULLIGAN FAVORITES
00843038..............$16.99

43. GERRY MULLIGAN CLASSICS
00843039..............$16.99

44. OLIVER NELSON
00843040..............$16.95

45. GEORGE GERSHWIN
00103643..............$24.99

46. BROADWAY JAZZ STANDARDS
00843042..............$15.99

47. CLASSIC JAZZ BALLADS
00843043..............$15.99

48. BEBOP CLASSICS
00843044..............$16.99

49. MILES DAVIS STANDARDS
00843045..............$16.95

50. GREAT JAZZ CLASSICS
00843046..............$15.99

51. UP-TEMPO JAZZ
00843047..............$15.99

52. STEVIE WONDER
00843048..............$16.99

53. RHYTHM CHANGES
00843049..............$15.99

54. "MOONLIGHT IN VERMONT" AND OTHER GREAT STANDARDS
00843050..............$15.99

55. BENNY GOLSON
00843052..............$15.95

56. "GEORGIA ON MY MIND" & OTHER SONGS BY HOAGY CARMICHAEL
00843056..............$15.99

57. VINCE GUARALDI
00843057..............$16.99

58. MORE LENNON AND MCCARTNEY
00843059..............$16.99

59. SOUL JAZZ
00843060..............$16.99

60. DEXTER GORDON
00843061..............$15.95

61. MONGO SANTAMARIA
00843062..............$15.95

62. JAZZ-ROCK FUSION
00843063..............$16.99

63. CLASSICAL JAZZ
00843064..............$14.95

64. TV TUNES
00843065..............$14.95

65. SMOOTH JAZZ
00843066..............$16.99